It's My State! ★ ★ ★ ★ ★ ★

Mississippi

The Magnolia State

Kerry Jones Waring and Ann Graham Gaines

Cavendish
Square

New York

Published in 2016 by Cavendish Square Publishing, LLC
243 5th Avenue, Suite 136, New York, NY 10016

Library of Congress Cataloging-in-Publication Data

Gaines, Ann.
Mississippi / Ann Graham Gaines and Kerry Jones Waring.
pages cm — (It's my state!)
Includes index.
ISBN 978-1-6271-3241-1 (hardcover) ISBN 978-1-6271-3243-5 (ebook)
1. Mississippi—History—Juvenile literature. I. Waring, Kerry Jones. II. Title.

F341.3.G352 2016
976.2—dc23

2015026235

Editorial Director: David McNamara
Editor: Fletcher Doyle
Copy Editor: Nathan Heidelberger
Art Director: Jeffrey Talbot
Designer: Stephanie Flecha
Senior Production Manager: Jennifer Ryder-Talbot
Production Editor: Renni Johnson
Photo Research: J8 Media

The photographs in this book are used by permission and through the courtesy of: Jon McIntosh/Getty Images, cover; Roksana Bashyrova/Thinkstock, 4; D. Robert &
Lorri Franz, 4; Daniel Prudek/Shutterstock.com, 4; Stuart Westmorland, 5; Ghedoghedo/File:Basilosaurus isis 3.JPG/Wikimedia Commons, 5; Valentyn Volkov/Shutterstock.
com, 5; MSMcCarthy Photography/Thinkstock, 6; Photri/Topham/The Image Works, 8; JayL/Shutterstock.com, 9; Accurate Art, 10; Clint Farlinger, 12; Raymond
Gehman, 13; Elizabeth Parker/Thinkstock, 14; Pearl River Resort, 14; Carol M. Highsmith Archive/Library of Congress/Prints and Photographs Division, 14; Csarsene/
File:Mississippi Petrified Forest.JPG/Wikimedia Commons, 15; Northeast Mississippi Daily Journal/Thomas Wells/AP Images, 15; Zack Frank/Shutterstock.com, 15; Cheryl
Casey/Shutterstock.com, 16; jgorzynik/Shutterstock.com, 19; Joe McDonald, 20; Tom & Pat Leeson, 20; Michael Durham, 20; Maurice Volmeyer/Shutterstock.com, 21;
Copyright Michael Forsberg/www.michaelforsberg.com, 21; Keneva Photography/Shutterstock.com, 21; Rob Hainer/Shutterstock.com, 22; Wikimedia Commons, 24;
Danny Lehman, 26; PoodlesRock, 28; MPI/Getty Images, 29; Carrin Campanelli Photography, 30; Billy Hathorn/File:Stanton Hall, Natchez, MS IMG 6989.JPG/Wikimedia
Commons, 32; SNEHIT/Shutterstock.com, 34; Woodlot/File:McLeodHouse (Hattiesburg, MS).JPG/Wikimedia Commons, 34; Katyrw/File:Grand Opera House Meridan
MS.JPG/Wikimedia Commons, 35; The Democrat-Times/Bill Johnson/AP Images, 35; © Look and Learn/Bridgeman Images, 36; Nik Wheeler, 37; Flip Schulke, 38; Marion
S. Trikosko/Library of Congress/Prints and Photographs Division, 39; Joe Raedle/Getty Images, 40; Pierre-Jean Durieu/Shutterstock.com, 44; Mississippi Development
Authority/Division of Tourism, 46; Fuse/Thinkstock, 47; Hulton Archive/Getty Images, 48; William Coupon, 48; Jason Merritt/Getty Images, 48; Reuters, 49; John Springer
Collection, 49; s_bukley/Shutterstock.com, 49; Accurate Art, 50; Philip Gould, 52; MCT via Getty Images, 54; John Fitzhugh/The Sun Herald/AP Images, 54; Rogelio V. Solis/
AP Images, 55; Main Street Corinth, 55; Dosfotos/Design Pics/Getty Images, 56; Flip Schulke/Corbis, 58; Christopher Halloran/Shutterstock.com, 59; Mary Knox Merrill/The
Christian Science Monitor/Getty Images, 60; Mathew B. Brady/Library of Congress/Prints and Photographs Division, 62; Andy Kuno/AP Images; 62; Office of the Clerk, U.S.
House of Representatives/File:Bennie Thompson Official portrait 107th Congress.JPG/Wikimedia Commons, 62; Paul J. Richards/AFP/Getty Images, 63; Simply Photos/
Shutterstock.com, 64; Owaki-Kulla, 66; Buddy Mays, 67; Philip Gould, 68; Richard Hamilton Smith, 68; Philip Gould, 69; Jeff Greenberg, 69; Sian Irvine/Dorling Kindersley/
Getty Images, 70; Dave G. Houser/Post-Housertock, 71; © Reuters/Corbis, 73; Mapping, 74; Thomas R. Machnitzki/File:Arkabutla Lake and Dam DeSoto and Tate Counties
MS 09.JPG/Wikimedia Commons, 75; Woodlot/File:LongleafPine.JPG/Wikimedia Commons, 75; Christopher Santoro, 76 (seal and flag).

MISSISSIPPI

CONTENTS

★ State Flower: Magnolia

In 1900, the magnolia blossom was voted in as state flower by Mississippi's schoolchildren. Students also voted for the magnolia tree in the early 1930s to become the state tree. Wild magnolia trees can grow to be 60 feet (18 meters) high or more. Their flowers, which blossom in the spring, come in white and cream.

★ State Bird: Mockingbird

The gray and white mockingbird, which is seen all over Mississippi, is a loud and energetic singer. The bird mimics the sounds of other birds and animals, and that is why "mocking" is part of its name. The mockingbird was selected as the state bird by the state legislature in 1944.

★ State Insect: Honeybee

Honeybees were designated as Mississippi's state insect in 1980. The honey they produce is often sold in Mississippi at farmers markets and roadside stands. Honeybees also help fruits and flowers grow through a process called pollination. Pollen is food for honeybees and also helps plants reproduce and spread.

MISSISSIPPI

State Water Mammal: Bottlenose Dolphin

The bottlenose dolphin lives off the coast of Mississippi in the Gulf of Mexico. A member of the whale family, the bottlenose has sharp teeth, a small snout, and a dorsal fin. It breathes through a blowhole located on top of its head.

State Fossil: Prehistoric Whale

Fifty million years ago, Mississippi was covered by an ocean that was filled with life. One of the most amazing creatures to swim in those waters was the prehistoric whale, also known as the *Basilosaurus*. In 1981, the Mississippi state government declared the prehistoric whale as the official state fossil.

State Shell: Oyster Shell

Oyster shells were made the state shell in 1974. Oysters live in brackish water in bays and sounds and in saltwater. Over the last decade, oyster populations along the Gulf Coast have been threatened by hurricanes, oil spills, and large amounts of freshwater from spillways designed to protect cities from flooding.

The Dunleith mansion in Natchez was built in 1856 on a plantation to replace a home that had burned down. It is now an inn and a National Historic Landmark.

The Magnolia State

C harley Pride, a famous country singer and member of the Grand Ole Opry, was born in the town of Sledge, in Mississippi. He once said of his home state, "I loved Mississippi and do to this day. The rainbows that stretch from horizon to horizon after a summer rain are the most spectacular I have ever seen." For a small state—just thirty-second in size compared with other US states—Mississippi's landscapes are spectacular. The state runs about 350 miles (563 kilometers) from north to south and 140 miles (225 km) from east to west. Within those 46,923 square miles (121,530 square kilometers) are rolling hills, slow-moving waterways called bayous, rushing streams, large and small rivers, farmland, sleepy towns, and several bustling cities.

Situated on the Gulf of Mexico, Mississippi is in a part of the United States that geographers call the Deep South. In terms of both geography and way of life, the state is often grouped with Louisiana, which sits to the west, and Alabama and Georgia, to the east.

Mississippi's shape looks much like a rectangle. The Mississippi River forms the state's western boundary. As the river weaves in and out, so does the state's western border. Louisiana cuts a small notch into Mississippi's rectangular shape.

A Rich Land

Three important physical features shape Mississippi's landscape. The first is the Appalachian Mountains, a long mountain chain that runs along the United States' Eastern Seaboard. One peak of the Appalachians, called Woodall Mountain, rises 806 feet (246 m) above sea level. This is Mississippi's highest point.

An even greater influence than the Appalachians on Mississippi's land is its major river. The Mississippi River begins as a narrow stream, just 20 to 30 feet (6 to 9 m) wide, up north in Minnesota. By the time its waters reach the state of Mississippi, almost 1,600 miles (2,575 km) later, the river is 2 miles (3.2 km) wide in some parts.

This satellite image of the Mississippi River Delta, about 100 miles (161 kilometers) below New Orleans, was taken in 2001.

For thousands of years, the river's ever-changing waters have built up a broad, flat **delta** in the western part of Mississippi. Also called an alluvial plain, the delta is an area where the river's floodwaters have deposited a thick layer of rich, black soil over the land.

Mississippi Borders

North:	Tennessee
South:	Gulf of Mexico
East:	Alabama
West:	Arkansas Louisiana

The Mississippi River has also created special water features called oxbow lakes. Many of these lakes formed naturally over long periods of time. As loops of the river became cut off from the rest of the river, they formed small, U-shaped lakes. Other oxbow lakes have formed when engineers reshaped the river with dams to control flooding.

To the south of the state lies the Gulf of Mexico. Measured in a straight line, Mississippi's coastline is 40 miles (64 km) long. However, its coastline is anything but straight. Many bays and coves cut into the land along the southern coastline. If you followed all the ins and outs of these inlets, you would discover that the shoreline actually measures around 350 miles (563 km). The pounding of the waves constantly reshapes the coastline. A chain of small islands along the shore offers some protection for the mainland from storms that blow in off the Gulf.

Mississippi's Waters

Abundant waterways make Mississippi a very green state. Rivers of all sizes flow across the land. While the Mississippi is the state's largest river, it is just one of many. The state also has numerous bayous. These marshy streams move so slowly, they hardly seem to move at all. Some bayous connect lakes and rivers in what is called the Delta Region of the state. Bayous to the south empty into inland waters and then into the Gulf of Mexico.

Through the western part of the state flow tributaries. These are other rivers that eventually empty into the Mississippi River. These tributaries include the Yalobusha and Tallahatchie Rivers, which meet just north of the city of Greenwood and form a single river, called the Yazoo. This important waterway runs south and west until it reaches the city of Vicksburg and the Mississippi River. Running a similar course, the Big Black River crosses the state from east to west before emptying into the Mississippi River.

A new bridge (*left*) carries cars and the Old Vicksburg Bridge carries trains across the Mississippi River into Louisiana.

MISSISSIPPI ★ ★ ★

COUNTY MAP

MISSISSIPPI
POPULATION BY COUNTY

County	Population	County	Population	County	Population
Adams	32,297	Itawamba	23,401	Pike	40,404
Alcorn	37,057	Jackson	139,668	Pontotoc	29,957
Amite	13,131	Jasper	17,062	Prentiss	25,276
Attala	19,564	Jefferson	7,726	Quitman	8,223
Benton	8,729	Jefferson Davis	12,487	Rankin	141,617
Bolivar	34,145	Jones	67,761	Scott	28,264
Calhoun	14,962	Kemper	10,456	Sharkey	4,916
Carroll	10,597	Lafayette	47,351	Simpson	27,503
Chickasaw	17,392	Lamar	55,658	Smith	16,491
Choctaw	8,547	Lauderdale	80,261	Stone	17,786
Claiborne	9,604	Lawrence	12,929	Sunflower	29,450
Clarke	16,732	Leake	23,805	Tallahatchie	15,378
Clay	20,634	Lee	82,910	Tate	28,886
Coahoma	26,151	Leflore	32,317	Tippah	22,232
Copiah	29,449	Lincoln	34,869	Tishomingo	19,593
Covington	19,568	Lowndes	59,779	Tunica	10,778
DeSoto	161,252	Madison	95,203	Union	27,134
Forrest	74,934	Marion	27,088	Walthall	15,443
Franklin	8,118	Marshall	37,144	Warren	48,773
George	22,578	Monroe	36,989	Washington	51,137
Greene	14,400	Montgomery	10,925	Wayne	20,747
Grenada	21,906	Neshoba	29,676	Webster	10,253
Hancock	43,929	Newton	21,720	Wilkinson	9,878
Harrison	187,105	Noxubee	11,545	Winston	19,198
Hinds	245,285	Oktibbeha	47,671	Yalobusha	12,678
Holmes	19,198	Panola	34,707	Yazoo	28,065
Humphreys	9,375	Pearl River	55,834		
Issaquena	1,406	Perry	12,250		

Source: US Bureau of the Census, 2010

The central and eastern parts of the state are covered by smaller rivers and creeks that grow in size as they run south toward the Gulf of Mexico. These include the Pascagoula and the Chickasawhay Rivers as well as the much larger Pearl River.

In the northeastern part of the state, the Tombigbee River runs south into Alabama, where it continues its course to the Gulf of Mexico.

Mississippi has many lakes, the largest of which have been created by damming rivers. Among such bodies of water are the Ross Barnett Reservoir on the Pearl River; Arkabutla Lake on the Coldwater River; Grenada Lake on the Yalobusha River; and the Pickwick Lake on the Tennessee River.

The Delta Region

Some geographers divide the state into two regions: the Alluvial Plain, or Delta, to the west, and the East Gulf Coastal Plain. However, Mississippians usually think of their state as having five distinct regions: the Delta Region, the Capital/River Region, the Hills Region, the Pines Region, and the Coastal Region.

The Delta Region is located between the Mississippi and the Yazoo Rivers. This flat area frequently floods and spreads a kind of soil called silt along the way. Rich soil in an area called the Bottomlands supports huge trees, luscious plants and vines, and many of

Paddlewheelers ferried passengers up the Mississippi River into the interior of the United States.

The Natchez Trace Parkway follows a historic trail that connected the city of Natchez with Nashville, Tennessee.

Mississippi's agricultural crops. Outcroppings called bluffs rise from the riverbanks in parts of the Delta Region where the Mississippi River has cut a path over time.

The Capital/River Region

Mississippians tend to refer to the southwestern corner of their state as the Capital/River Region. The area, bound by the Mississippi River on the west and the Pearl River on the east, stretches south to the dividing line between Mississippi and Louisiana. The cities of Vicksburg and Jackson are on the northern border of the area. The Capital/River Region looks much like the Delta Region, with river bluffs, flatland, and many bayous and oxbow lakes. However, the Capital/River Region is much more heavily populated.

One population center of the region is Jackson. It is not only the state's capital but also Mississippi's largest city. Suburbs and small towns have grown up around Jackson. Parts of the region look like places all across the United States, with housing developments, strip malls, and parking lots. Not all of the construction in this area is modern, however. In some parts of Jackson, historical Southern architecture has been preserved.

Elvis Presley's Birthplace

Geyser Falls Water Theme Park

Longwood

1. Buccaneer State Park

This park has natural settings, including forests and marshlands, and man-made fun like Buccaneer Bay Waterpark. General Andrew Jackson used the site as a base during the War of 1812. It suffered heavy damage during Hurricane Katrina in 2005.

2. Delta Blues Museum

The style of music called "the blues" is one of Mississippi's many cultural landmarks. The Delta Blues Museum in Clarksdale is the place to explore the history of this art form and to take music classes year-round.

3. Elvis Presley Birthplace and Museum

Tupelo is the birthplace of Elvis Presley, the King of Rock and Roll. Visitors can see the house Presley was raised in, view artifacts from his life, and hear live music in the museum's theater.

4. Geyser Falls Water Theme Park

This water park is the place to beat the Mississippi heat with thirteen water slides, including a six-story freefall slide. A wave pool, lazy river, and 8 acres (3.2 hectares) of sand on Clearwater Key beach are other attractions.

5. Longwood

This house museum in Natchez is also called Nutt's Folly after its original owner, Dr. Haller Nutt. Construction of the unique eight-sided mansion was halted and never completed after the start of the Civil War in 1861.

6. Mississippi Petrified Forest

Visitors to this National Natural Landmark can view petrified, or fossilized, trees that are millions of years old. Evidence shows that the forest near the town of Flora was formed by a combination of natural events, including flooding and the action of glaciers.

7. Old Capitol Museum

Once called the State House, this historic building served as the state capitol from 1839 to 1903. It also was used as a state office building before being converted to a museum in 1961. The building was restored between 2007 and 2009.

8. Tupelo Automobile Museum

More than one hundred antique cars are on display at the Tupelo Automobile Museum, ranging from an 1886 Benz to a Dodge Viper built in 1994. A Lincoln owned by Elvis Presley is part of the collection.

9. Vicksburg National Military Park

The site of the Civil War's Battle of Vicksburg has more monuments than nearly any other military park in the world—1,330 monuments, markers, tablets, and plaques. Vicksburg National Cemetery is located here.

10. Walter Anderson Museum of Art

Walter Anderson is known for his paintings of the plants, animals, and people of the Gulf Coast. This museum, opened in 1991 in Ocean Springs, celebrates his works and those of his brothers, Peter Anderson and James McConnell Anderson.

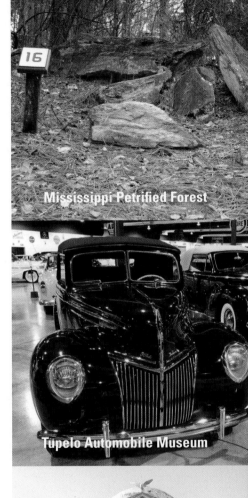

Mississippi Petrified Forest

Tupelo Automobile Museum

Vicksburg National Military Park

The Hills Region

In the northeastern part of the state is a hilly section called the Hills Region. In the extreme northeastern corner of the Hills Region are the sandy Tennessee River Hills. To the west, in the center of this area, is Pontotoc Ridge. The Appalachian Mountains begin their rise in the north, stretching into Tennessee. Much of this part of the Hills Region is wooded. The federal government established two national forests here. Some of the towns in this region are Corinth, Oxford, and Tupelo, the birthplace of Elvis Presley.

The Pines Region

Early explorers describe the area that is now Mississippi as a forested land. Today, a broad band of piney woods cuts across the center of the state, which Mississippians call the Pines Region. This area stretches from the Hills Region up to the coastal plain. Lumbering and farming centers lie in cleared areas of these forests. Like the Delta to its west and the Hills to its north, this region is sparsely populated.

The Coastal Region

To the south of the Pines Region is the Coastal Region along the Gulf of Mexico. A string of islands lies offshore in the Gulf of Mexico. In 1969, Hurricane Camille split Ship Island

Volunteers worked hard to restore Mississippi's white-sand beaches after the *Deepwater Horizon* oil spill in 2010.

in two. One half of the former island is now called East Ship Island. It is a place where ships have anchored ever since the British Navy stayed there during the War of 1812.

The part of the Gulf that lies between these coastal islands and the rest of the state is called the Mississippi Sound, a long and shallow body of water. There are large bays at the towns of Bay St. Louis and Pascagoula. As the Pearl and Pascagoula Rivers flow into the sound, they form wide deltas with marshes and swampland.

In this region are the old port cities of Biloxi, Gulfport, Pascagoula, and Bienville. Visitors flock to the white beaches along Mississippi's shoreline with its many resorts and campgrounds. Just up from the coast, a series of sand steps or terraces have formed from sand that blows in from the Gulf.

Climate

Mississippi's rivers, lakes, bayous, ocean, and warm climate make it a hot, humid place for much of the year. Temperatures seldom dip below 40 degrees Fahrenheit (4.4 degrees Celsius) in the winter, but reach an average of around 92°F (33.3°C) in the summer.

Hurricanes regularly threaten the state, especially along its Gulf Coast. Hurricane Camille hit Mississippi hard in 1969. However, even people who survived Camille agree that Hurricane Katrina hit harder when it roared into Mississippi on August 29, 2005. Winds measured 145 miles per hour (233 kilometers per hour) when Katrina made landfall in Louisiana. That made it one of the strongest hurricanes ever to hit the United States. After making landfall, the hurricane skipped along the shore a little farther east. It came ashore for a second time, this time at the Louisiana/Mississippi border. The winds had decreased a little, but they still measured 125 miles per hour (201 kmh). Not only did the wind cause great damage but so did a huge storm surge. This powerful moving wall of water rushed into Mississippi's coastal cities. Most of the buildings along the shore were wiped out or heavily damaged. One storm surge near the town of Pass Christian measured 27.8 feet (8.5 m), making it the largest ever recorded in the United States. Katrina's winds and storm surges also caused great damage to Waveland, Bay St. Louis, Long Beach, Gulfport, Ocean Springs, Gautier, and Pascagoula.

In addition to the devastating hurricane, eleven tornadoes accompanied Katrina in Mississippi. Two of them were rated as F2 on the Fujita scale. That means the tornadoes caused significant damage and packed winds of anywhere between 113 and 157 miles per hour (182 to 253 kmh).

When the storm had passed, more than two hundred people in Mississippi had been killed and thousands of homes and businesses had been destroyed. Affected families had to find temporary places to live in shelters, trailers, and in the homes of relatives or even strangers who lived in safer areas. When President George W. Bush toured the state in May 2006, he expressed admiration for the people of the state who were working hard to rebuild. He said that Mississippians showed "a strength that wind and water can never take away."

Each year brings the possibility of hurricanes and tornadoes to the state. However, the people of Mississippi continue to come up with new ways to protect themselves from danger. For example, after Hurricane Katrina, buildings and bridges were rebuilt to be stronger than they were before. The emergency command centers along the coast had been flooded during the storm, so they were rebuilt on higher ground. A new coastal Mississippi is on the way!

Mississippi's Wild Places

In a state where more than half the land is covered with forest, there is something for every nature lover. The forested areas are filled with a variety of trees, wildlife, and wildflowers.

The northern forests of Mississippi support hardwoods, including elm, hickory, and oak, as well as evergreens. The town of Tupelo is named after a special gum tree that flourishes in swamps and other wet places. Several kinds of pine trees—the longleaf, slash pine, and loblolly—grow mainly in the south.

White-tailed deer live all across the state, often moving out from the forests into populated areas. Mississippi's forests and fields are also home to wild hogs, black bears, squirrels, foxes, opossums, rabbits, raccoons, and skunks.

Mississippi's forests shelter a variety of birds, such as eastern wild turkeys, bobwhite quails, mourning doves, and woodcocks. Birdwatchers thrill at the sight of the red-cockaded woodpecker, a bird that is on the rare and endangered species list.

Black-eyed Susans bloom from June to October in Mississippi's warm climate.

Mississippi's wildflowers and tree blossoms burst into color in the spring. These flowers include pink and red wild azaleas; creamy magnolias; black-eyed Susans; pale pink camellias; purple and white irises; pink and white dogwood blossoms; violets; tiny trillium flowers in whites, yellows, and reds; and the ivory Cherokee rose, which Native Americans first cultivated in the area.

Mississippi's wild wetlands also shelter large numbers of animals and birds. Millions of water birds such as ducks, geese, and swans live in rivers, streams, and bayous. Egrets, herons, and terns nest along the coastal shorelines and the banks of Mississippi's rivers and lakes. Alligators, snapping turtles, and water snakes, including the **venomous**, or poisonous, cottonmouth, populate the state's waterways. Bass, bream, catfish, croaker, and perch swim in Mississippi's fresh waters. Other creatures found in coastal waters include saltwater fish such as mackerel, menhaden, and big tarpon, as well as crabs, oysters, and shrimp.

The state of Mississippi protects a number of its endangered animals. Black bears, Florida panthers, gray bats, Indiana bats, sea turtles, gopher tortoises, sawback turtles (also called map turtles; black-knobbed, ringed, and yellow-blotched), black pine snakes, eastern indigo snakes, rainbow snakes, and southern hognose snakes are on the endangered animals list in Mississippi.

★10★KEY PLANTS AND ANIMALS

American Alligator

Black Bear

Pitcher Plant

1. American Alligator

American alligators were endangered but their numbers are growing. In 2005, the American alligator was declared Mississippi's state reptile. Male alligators grow up to 15 feet (4.6 m) long, and the average gator has seventy-five teeth.

2. Bald Cypress

Ancient forests of bald cypresses once grew in swamp water or near the Mississippi River. Many of these trees have been cut down for their valuable timber. They have knobby roots, and they have needles rather than leaves.

3. Black Bear

These small bears nearly died out in Mississippi due to excessive hunting and the disappearance of hardwood forests. In 2002, wildlife experts estimated there were fewer than fifty bears in the state. Since then, they believe that number has more than doubled.

4. Flame Azalea

This rare native plant has dramatic orange, yellow, and red flowers and a sweet fragrance. The flame azalea blooms in late spring and produces flowers before leaves. It can reach a height of 10 feet (3 m). Its habitat is threatened by development.

5. Pitcher Plant

Pitcher plants grow in the damp bogs of Mississippi. These plants can hold liquid and devour insects. The plant's sweet nectar attracts insects into its tube-shaped leaves, where they become trapped in the hairs that cover the leaf's interior.

6. River Otter

River otters help keep their ecosystem in balance. Preservation scientists look for the presence of these animals to determine water quality. If otters are found, the river is healthy enough to support a range of plants and animals.

River Otter

7. Sandhill Crane

Mississippi's sandhill cranes are an endangered species. They stand about 4 feet (1.2 m) tall, have a nearly 6-foot (1.8 m) wingspan, and have long legs and necks. They have gray feathers, a red crown, white cheek patches, and black legs.

8. Virginia Wildrye

Virgina wildrye is a kind of grass. Deer, cows, and sheep eat it, and small mammals forage for its seeds. Its color may range from green to silvery blue and it can grow to 5 feet (1.5 m) tall.

Sandhill Crane

9. Wild Turkey

In the early 1900s, wild turkeys were nearly hunted to extinction. Because of the efforts of wildlife experts, the state's turkey population grew to about four hundred thousand in the 1980s, though it has been on the decline again in recent years.

10. Yellow Coneflower

These striking plants are native to lands west of the Mississippi River. The stems can be 2 to 3 feet (0.6 to 0.9 m) tall, and its yellow or orange petals tend to point down from the center of the flower.

Wild Turkey

The Biloxi Lighthouse was built in 1848. It was damaged by Hurricane Katrina in 2005 but withstood a storm surge that covered the lower third of the 64-foot (19.5 m) structure in seawater.

From the Beginning

Thousands of years ago, humans came to live on the land that would one day become Mississippi. The land was an ideal place for these hunting and gathering people to settle. Its many rivers provided water to drink, fish to eat, and an easy way to travel and trade goods. The forests were full of animals to hunt for food and wood to use for building simple shelters and dugout canoes. These early people soon discovered that they did not always have to hunt animals and gather fruit and nuts for all their food. They could stay and grow some of the food they needed in the area's rich soil.

The Mississippi River gave these early groups so much that many of them considered it to be the center of the universe. **Archaeologists,** the scientists who study the past, have found evidence that these early people built small cities and farming communities in several areas of the land that is now Mississippi. The archaeologists have unearthed stone and metal tools, weapons, pottery, masks, and engraved seashells that indicate busy, successful communities. These experts believe that the ancient people they call Mound Builders built the huge mounds of earth located around Mississippi and other nearby states. These early people probably honored their leaders and their dead by building homes and temples on the flat tops of some of these mounds.

Mound Builders from the Mississippian culture constructed this mound in Illinois and others like it in Mississippi.

Native Americans

It is believed that over time the descendants of the Mound Builders organized themselves into separate villages and groups. These communities survived by hunting, fishing, and farming. The people used dugout canoes to travel and trade along the coastal shores and on the rivers. They probably lived in shelters made of leaves and wooden poles or log houses plastered with clay from nearby riverbanks. Living in separate areas, these individual communities eventually developed their own languages and customs.

One such group was the Chickasaw. Some experts believe the Chickasaw and the Choctaw may have been part of one group in earlier times. Spread across Mississippi, Alabama, Tennessee, and Kentucky, the Chickasaw were seminomadic. They moved part of the time and settled along waterways within their territory at other times. Members

Biloxi Light

This well-known lighthouse in Biloxi is located on Mississippi Sound. It has been kept by female lighthouse keepers for longer than any other lighthouse in the United States. The lighthouse has been damaged by a number of hurricanes, including Camille and Katrina.

of their group hunted, gathered, and grew enough food to feed their own people. Chickasaw society was well organized, with strong leaders and good lines of communication. Runners carried messages along the Chickasaw network to far-scattered people whenever they needed to hold a meeting, or council. Chickasaw defenses were so strong that they boasted their members were almost never captured or killed.

Legacy of War

During the Civil War, Jackson was taken over by Union forces and almost completely burned down. The city was nicknamed "Chimneyville" because only the chimneys of most buildings were left standing. As a result, few pre-war structures exist there today.

To the south and east into Alabama lived the Choctaw, a forest people who also farmed and traded. Like the other groups in the area, the Choctaw were well organized. Their central government included courts where elders could listen to group members' complaints and settle them. Many Choctaw males had sloping flat foreheads. **Ethnologists** believe members of the group pressed boards against male babies' foreheads to give them their distinctive shape. This made them identifiable as Choctaw and set them apart from the men of other Native groups. Early European explorers noted that the Choctaw were fast runners who also loved to play ball games. Players sometimes peacefully settled disputes with other groups by playing stickball.

The Natchez people lived along the Mississippi River. At least five hundred years ago, they used the river's waters and rich bottomlands to grow corn, squash, and beans. They organized their society into separate classes of nobility (rulers) and commoners (ordinary people). The Natchez had one supreme ruler, called the Great Sun, who was so honored that he was carried everywhere so he never had to touch the ground. Though many Native American groups who lived close to each other spoke related languages, the Natchez spoke a distinct language that has few close relatives.

Many of the place names in Mississippi, such as Biloxi, Yazoo, and Pascagoula, come from Native American languages. According to Muriel H. Wright, a historian who wrote a book about the history of the Mississippi River, the Chippewa word "Mississippi" has been translated as "great river" or "gathering of waters." According to Choctaw legend, when their ancestors came upon the river, they exclaimed, "*Misha sipokni*!" That phrase has been translated as, "Here is a river that is beyond all age!"

The Native People

When European settlers arrived in the area that became known as Mississippi, there were eight main tribes of Native Americans living there: the Biloxi, the Chickasaw, the Choctaw, the Houma, the Natchez, the Ofo, the Quapaw, and the Tunica.

The Native American tribes living in Mississippi had many things in common. Most lived in houses made of rivercane frames and covered with plaster and thatched roofs. These houses are sometimes called wattle and daub houses. Often, small villages of these houses would be surrounded by a structure called a palisade that protected the group from attack. Most of these tribes were farming people, and they grew corn, beans, and squash to live off. They built canoes by digging out logs. They also hunted deer and turkey and fished in the abundant waters of the Gulf Coast using spears, harpoons, and nets. The women collected nuts, fruits, and mushrooms. Most of the men wore breechcloths and leggings, and the women often wore wraparound skirts. Most of their clothes were made of deerskin or other animal hide. Many of these tribes coexisted peacefully and traded with each other. Most tribes had their own language. The Native Americans in this region created many distinct works of art and crafts, including pottery, baskets, and wood carvings.

Like many other parts of the United States, the arrival of European settlers brought great changes to the Native American tribes of Mississippi. Diseases brought by colonists, including cholera, smallpox, influenza, and tuberculosis, caused the deaths of many Native Americans. The Biloxi tribe was nearly wiped out by a smallpox epidemic. The surviving

The Grand Village of the Natchez displays reconstructions of the grass and clay homes built by the Natchez people.

members of the tribe moved west and joined the Tunica tribe. Around 1720, the Natchez people staged a revolt against French settlers after the settlers seized some of their land. The resulting warfare lasted most of next few decades. Some Chickasaw and Choctaw tribes fought alongside the French to drive the Natchez off their land. By approximately 1740, the Natchez were mostly disbanded and scattered. Many joined other tribes such as the Cherokee and Creek people.

Today, the only federally recognized tribe in Mississippi is the Mississippi Band of Choctaw Indians.

Spotlight on the Chickasaw

The name of the Chickasaw tribe is derived from Chikasha, the name of a legendary Chickasaw leader.

Distribution: In addition to Mississippi, many Chickasaw also lived in Alabama, Tennessee, Kentucky, and Missouri. After the arrival of European settlers, many Chickasaw were forced to move to Oklahoma.

Homes: The Chickasaw traditionally lived in small villages and farming communities. Their homes, called wattle and daub houses, were made of rivercane and plaster with thatched roofs. The Chickasaw often built reinforced walls made from tree trunks around their villages to protect them.

Food: Most of the Chickasaw's food came from farming. They grew beans, squash, pumpkins, and corn. They also gathered nuts, berries, and fruit. The men of the tribe hunted for wild turkey and deer and fished in rivers and along the coast.

Government: Historically, the Chickasaw people were governed by a council of chiefs led by a war chief called a *minko*. The minko made military and political decisions for the tribe. Today, the Chickasaw have an elected council and governor, though they also follow the laws of the United States.

Clothing: Most Chickasaw clothing was made out of animal skin, usually deer. The men wore breechcloths and, when the weather was cold, leggings. The women wore skirts and sometimes poncho-style blouses. Both men and women wore moccasins.

Art: The Chickasaw people were known for making baskets out of rivercane, as well as making wood carvings, textiles, and pottery.

Natives and Europeans Meet

The Spanish explorer Hernando de Soto and an army of several hundred soldiers became the first Europeans to see what is now the state of Mississippi. Searching for treasure in 1540, the members of this expedition began their explorations in Florida and ended beyond the Rio Grande in the Southwest. When de Soto's group passed through the area that is present-day Mississippi, it encountered members of three Native American nations: the Natchez, the Choctaw, and the Chickasaw. The Chickasaw were the people with whom de Soto had the most contact. The Chickasaw did not welcome the contact, though. They attacked de Soto's party several times until the Spaniards left the area.

In 1673, 130 years after de Soto's visit to America, the French explorers Jacques Marquette and Louis Jolliet came down the Mississippi River. They turned around when they reached a village at the mouth of the Arkansas River, populated by Native Americans called the Arkansas. The two explorers did not travel any farther because they feared meeting enemy Spaniards, who were also exploring the area.

In 1682, a French explorer called René-Robert Cavelier, sieur de La Salle also traveled down the Mississippi River to the Gulf of Mexico. La Salle recorded meeting people

This painting by William Powell depicts Hernando de Soto and his men becoming the first Europeans to see the Mississippi River in 1541.

In the French and Indian War, the losing French lost all land east of the Mississippi River, including much of what is today the Magnolia State.

of the Taensa, Natchez, and Choctaw groups. When La Salle reached the mouth of the Mississippi, he claimed all the land along the huge river on behalf of his ruler, King Louis XIV of France.

In the years that followed, the French made several efforts to create colonies on the land La Salle had claimed. They wanted to prevent their Spanish rivals to the south from gaining complete control of the land that would eventually become the southern part of the United States. In 1699, Pierre Le Moyne d'Iberville brought two hundred settlers to a location in what is the present-day Bay of Biloxi. The group built Fort Maurepas. According to Iberville's plans, this would become the first capital of French Louisiana.

Eventually, the French built several plantations around Fort Maurepas. In 1719, the plantation owners imported slaves from Africa and forced these slaves to work without pay in the cotton, tobacco, rice, and indigo fields.

In the meantime, the British had also started colonies in North America. That led to conflicts with the French. Soon the British and French engaged in what would be called the French and Indian War, which lasted from 1754 to 1763. The name of the French and Indian War refers to fighting that occurred between the French, who were supported by their Native American allies, and the British, who had their own Native American allies.

Making a Tissue Box Guitar

Mississippi is famous for the many talented blues, country, and rock 'n' roll musicians who have called the state home. Follow these instructions to make your own guitar and play some music of your own.

What You Need

1 empty tissue box (the long, rectangular kind)
1 empty paper towel tube
3 or 4 rubber bands
Tape

Scissors
Marker/Pen
Stickers, paint, markers to decorate the box

What To Do

- Cut the clear cellophane (plastic) part off the tissue box opening.
- Pick the end of the box you're going to use for your guitar neck. Place your paper towel tube on that end and trace around it with your marker to draw a circle.
- Use your scissors to cut out the hole. This may be tricky to cut, so ask an adult for help if you need it.
- Insert the paper towel tube into the hole. If it won't stay on its own, use some tape to hold it in place.

- Make your guitar strings by stretching the rubber bands the long way around the box in front of the tissue box opening. You can include a string down the center by cutting a slit where the neck tube meets the box and sliding the rubber band into it before stretching it over the box.
- Decorate your guitar with stickers, markers, or glitter—or any other decorations you choose!
- Pluck your guitar strings to hear the noise they make. Now you're ready to make some music!

After the British defeated the French, Great Britain gained all of France's territories east of the Mississippi River, with the exception of the city of New Orleans. British government officials in London made southern Mississippi part of the British colony of West Florida. Northern Mississippi became part of Britain's Georgia colony.

Meanwhile, trouble was brewing in the British colonies. In 1775, many colonists became frustrated with the British rulers and began the American Revolution. However, the people who lived in what is now Mississippi did not become involved in the fighting of that war. Most residents of West Florida were Loyalists, or **Tories**, who remained loyal to Britain's King George III. They hoped the British would win the war. In 1781, the war directly affected the people of West Florida. Spain took control of West Florida while the British were fighting both the French and the Continental Army. When the Revolution came to an end two years later, the colonies separated from Great Britain and became the United States. Great Britain formally recognized Spain as West Florida's owner. Spain granted some northern land to the newly formed United States. In 1795, a new treaty moved West Florida's northern boundary south. The old boundary ran on a line starting at the point the Yazoo River ran into the Mississippi River. The new boundary was along an east–west line that ran roughly through Mobile, Alabama. This meant that most of present-day Mississippi became part of the United States.

The Mississippi Territory

In 1798, the US federal government organized this newly acquired land into the Mississippi Territory. This territory reached from the Chattahoochee River on the east to the Mississippi River on the west. The territory included about half of the present-day states of Alabama and Mississippi. The territory would grow twice more in less than twenty years.

In 1803, the United States expanded when President Thomas Jefferson completed the **Louisiana Purchase**. That added about 827,000 square miles (2,071,990 sq km) of western land to the United States, including the city of New Orleans. Americans became more

The free labor of slaves generated the money needed to build mansions such as Stanton Hall in Natchez.

involved in trade up and down the Mississippi River. One year later, Georgia ceded the land west of the Chattahoochee to the United States. The United States government then extended the territory's boundary farther north to the southern border of Tennessee.

In 1810, British settlers in West Florida rejected Spanish rule and declared themselves the independent Republic of West Florida. However, President James Madison had other ideas. He soon annexed the area and made the republic part of the United States. By 1813, the Mississippi Territory contained all of present-day Alabama and Mississippi.

Statehood

Traders and trappers were the first main groups to migrate to the Mississippi Territory, followed by herders and then farmers. The large amount of cheap land that was ideal for growing cotton in the new territory attracted many settlers. Most came from Georgia or North or South Carolina. Some left tobacco-growing areas because at the time, many tobacco farmers were struggling to make a profit. A steady migration began after the War of 1812, spurred by high prices for cotton, improved roads, and newly acquired outlets to the Gulf of Mexico. By 1817, the population of the Mississippi Territory had grown so much that the federal government divided it in two. The western half was admitted into the Union as the state of Mississippi on December 10. The eastern half became the Alabama Territory, which would become a state in 1819.

To do the backbreaking work of growing cotton in ever-larger fields, plantation owners continued to buy more and more slaves. Cotton had soon made Mississippi one of the richest states in the Union. Several wealthy white families lived in huge plantation homes or in elegant mansions in the busy, cultured city of Natchez. However, Mississippi had many more white families who farmed small pieces of land or ran small businesses.

Mississippi's large black population included a few hundred free blacks who lived and worked in the state. The slave population, however, numbered in the tens of thousands. Natchez had the second-largest slave market in the United States, where about two hundred thousand slaves were bought and sold.

The lives of slaves were largely ones of endless work. Owners sometimes split up slave families and sold the children to other plantations. Slaves often lived in broken-down cabins. They lacked basic necessities, such as enough food and clothing.

The Civil War

By the middle of the 1800s, Americans were involved in a heated **debate** about whether the practice of slavery should expand in the United States. Many people in the South wanted slavery to continue and grow. They believed their economy depended on it. They thought their region could not prosper without the free labor of slaves. Many people in the North, on the other hand, wanted to ban the import, sale, and use of slaves. This argument over slavery and another fight over states' rights caused the Civil War, which began in 1861. That is when Southern states voted to **secede**, or withdraw, from the Union. South Carolina was the first to do so. On January 9, 1861, Mississippi became the second state to secede. The Southern states then formed their own new nation, which they called the Confederate States of America. The Civil War began with the Battle of Fort Sumter in South Carolina on April 12, 1861.

The Civil War was a devastating period for Mississippi. The Union and

Cultural History

For much of the twentieth century, Greenville was home to Mississippi's largest Jewish community. Many immigrants found acceptance there in the late 1800s and early 1900s. Jewish people built successful businesses and maintained an active role in local government. Jewish heritage continues to be celebrated in Greenville.

10 KEY CITIES

Jackson

Hattiesburg

1. Jackson: population 173,514

Mississippi's largest city is also its capital. The city was named after President Andrew Jackson. Its historical and lively music scene offers live performances of the blues, gospel, and rock and roll.

2. Gulfport: population 67,793

Gulfport is located very close to Biloxi, and the area is often referred to as the Gulfport-Biloxi metropolitan area. The city was founded as a port for the lumber trade. It suffered a great amount of damage from Hurricane Katrina in 2005.

3. Southaven: population 48,982

Mississippi's third-largest city is considered a suburb of a city in another state—Memphis, Tennessee. Southaven was annexed, or officially established, in 1980 and is one of the fastest-growing cities in the Southeast.

4. Hattiesburg: population 45,989

Hattiesburg earned its nickname "the Hub City" in 1912 because it was located at the intersection of a number of railroad lines. The nickname holds true as a number of US and state highways run nearby. It is home to the University of Southern Mississippi.

5. Biloxi: population 44,054

Biloxi's beachfront lies on Mississippi Sound. Keesler Air Force Base, where US Air Force members receive technical training, is located here. Biloxi was once the third-largest city in Mississippi, but many people moved away after Hurricane Katrina.

★ MISSISSIPPI ★ ★ ★

6. Meridian: population 41,148

Meridian was established in 1860 as a trading center, as it was located at the intersection of the Mobile and Ohio Railroad and the Southern Railway. Much of the city was burned down during the Civil War and rebuilt.

7. Tupelo: population 34,546

Tupelo was the site of a key battle in the Civil War and is well known as the birthplace of Elvis Presley. As a baby in 1936, Presley survived one of the deadliest tornadoes in US history in Tupelo.

8. Greenville: population 34,400

The Queen City of the Delta has a rich history. Visitors can see the area's many Native American sites; eat Southern cooking; or walk the Mississippi **Levee** System, which is longer than the Great Wall of China.

9. Olive Branch: population 33,484

Olive Branch is a rapidly growing suburb of Memphis. A railroad line, first built in 1885, runs through Olive Branch and connects Memphis to Birmingham, Alabama. Olive Branch also has one of the busiest airports in Mississippi.

10. Horn Lake: population 26,066

Horn Lake is named for a nearby body of water shaped like a cow horn that formed after the Mississippi River changed course in the late eighteenth century. Elvis Presley's vacation home there is a tourist draw.

Meridian

Greenville

The Siege of Vicksburg, a painting by Angus McBride of Britain, depicts the bombardment of the city by Union gunboats.

Confederate armies fought many important battles in the state. A ferocious battle took place at Vicksburg when Union soldiers occupied the city after a forty-seven-day siege. The Union soldiers took over the port and destroyed businesses, churches, and homes. Confederate soldiers fought hard to defend Vicksburg during the siege. Without incoming food, supplies, and reinforcements, though, Confederate soldiers in Vicksburg finally surrendered on July 4, 1863.

Of the seventy-eight thousand Mississippi men and boys who fought for the Confederate army, approximately twelve thousand died in battle and fifteen thousand died of disease. The rest had been weakened by their lack of food, warm clothing, and shoes. The women, children, and old people who remained at home also suffered terribly. Many women took on the kind of hard, physical work formerly done by men. Like the soldiers, the women endured hunger, poverty, and sickness.

Mississippi's black population suffered during the Civil War as well. However, their future seemed brighter when President Abraham Lincoln declared all slaves to be free.

While Lincoln's Emancipation Proclamation in 1863 did free the slaves, life was still hard. There were few jobs to be had during or after the war for people of color. Like many white families, black families found it difficult to feed, house, and clothe themselves.

After the Civil War

Hard times continued in Mississippi in the years after the Civil War. The US government declared that the Southern states could reenter the Union, but first these states had to undergo reconstruction. Under reconstruction, the Southern states had to recognize the Fourteenth Amendment, which guarantees equal legal rights to all citizens; deny secession; and cancel debts owed to the Confederacy. The US government used its army to run the Southern states. It placed all of them, including Mississippi, under military law. The federal government told the Southern states when elections would be held and dictated who could run for office.

During the Reconstruction Era (1865–1877), Mississippi drew up a new state constitution. The constitution gave African Americans the right to vote and to hold

Sharecroppers faced long days of hard labor and struggled to make a living.

political office. It also made all children eligible for free public education. Although black Mississippians enjoyed newfound freedoms for a time, those liberties did not last. After Mississippi was formally readmitted to the Union, white politicians worked to regain the political power they had lost. They passed a new constitution that denied the state's black population many basic rights, such as the right to vote and the right to own property.

Change Comes Slowly

Mississippi's economy remained devastated for many decades after the Civil War. Without slave labor, the state never became rich from cotton again. After many big plantations fell into ruin, small farmers struggled to grow crops they could sell for a decent profit.

James Meredith's March Against Fear in 1966, which ended at the Mississippi State Capitol, encouraged four thousand African Americans in Mississippi to register to vote.

These small farmers, called **sharecroppers**, leased land from large landowners to whom they had to pay part of every crop. This tenant farm system made it hard for sharecroppers to get ahead financially. For decades, Mississippi remained one of the poorest states in the United States.

More hard times were on the way. In 1927, a devastating flood caused tens of thousands of Mississippians to leave their homes. When the country entered the Great Depression in 1929, Mississippians suffered even more. Many of them found it so hard to earn a living that they fled Mississippi. They headed north, hoping to find work in factories in cities such as New York City, Philadelphia, and Chicago. Times were tough across the country, though. Many businesses closed and many people lost their jobs. The government established programs to help the unemployed. The economy also improved when the country entered World War II. Workers were hired to make the supplies that were needed for the war effort.

James Meredith needed the protection of US Marshalls to enter classes at the University of Mississippi.

During this time, many blacks left Mississippi to escape racism. State laws kept **segregation** in place in Mississippi until well into the 1960s. Segregation laws stated that black people could not use the same facilities as whites. African Americans could not eat in certain restaurants or attend the same schools as whites. In addition, African Americans continued to be denied the right to vote.

Beginning in the late 1950s, individuals began to fight this unfair system and the civil rights movement got under way. In the 1960s, tensions grew in Mississippi between people who wanted to work for equality and those who wanted to keep segregation laws. In 1961, a young black man named James Meredith applied to the University of Mississippi, which had never admitted an African American. Meredith spent nine years in the US Air Force and several years at Jackson State College before applying to the university. He was accepted, but then was denied entry when officials at the university discovered his race. Race riots broke out after Meredith tried to become the first black student to register for classes on September 20, 1962. When President John F. Kennedy sent federal troops to try to stop the riots, the troops came under attack. Meredith sued, alleging discrimination, and officially enrolled on October 1. He later earned a law degree from Columbia University.

Oil-coated booms used to contain the *Deepwater Horizon* spill wash up on the beach at Waveland in 2010.

In 1965, the passage of the Voting Rights Act by Congress meant that Mississippi state officials could no longer deny African Americans the chance to vote. From that point on, Mississippi's black population steadily gained political power. In 1969, the Supreme Court ruled in favor of desegregation in a case involving thirty-three Mississippi school districts. The decision, *Alexander v. Holmes County Board of Education*, meant both black and white children had to attend the same schools. Desegregation did not go well at first. Many white parents removed their children from public schools and sent them to private schools instead. At the same time, the number of black school principals and teachers actually declined, as parents pressured schools to hire whites only. However, many educational reforms took place in the 1980s, and the quality of public education in Mississippi improved.

Mississippi's economy also grew in the 1980s and the 1990s. Agriculture became more varied and no longer depended so heavily on cotton. The state also began to promote tourism and invited visitors to enjoy its wild natural areas and historic sites. Tourism created many new jobs in hotels, restaurants, parks, historic sites, and riverboat casinos.

Natural and man-made disasters had a major impact on Mississippi life in the 2000s. Hurricane Katrina in 2005 was one of the most devastating storms to ever hit the Gulf Coast. The storm reached Mississippi's coastline on August 29, 2005. Many coastal towns in Mississippi and Louisiana were destroyed in one night. Hurricane force winds lasted over seventeen hours and led to eleven tornadoes and a 28-foot (8.5 m) storm surge. In addition to the deaths of more than 235 residents of the state, forty-nine counties in Mississippi were declared federal disaster areas, a designation that means there is enough damage to qualify for assistance from the federal government. Many historical buildings were destroyed, including the home of Jefferson Davis, the president of the Confederate States of America. Hundreds of Civil War artifacts were lost there. Biloxi, the largest city on Mississippi's coast, was hit particularly hard by the storm. Homes were leveled and a low-lying area called Point Cadet was completely wiped out. Several floating casino **barges** that had been in the waters surrounding Biloxi were washed onto land. One was found resting on Highway 90. The damage to Mississippi caused by Hurricane Katrina took years to repair. In some cases, rebuilding is still happening. However, many lessons were learned from the storm. Bridges were rebuilt taller and stronger. Emergency response plans were improved. Hurricane Katrina had a long-lasting impact on the Gulf Coast, but the residents there continue to work toward restoring their towns and cities to their original state.

In 2010, disaster struck the Gulf Coast once more. On April 20, an oil rig named *Deepwater Horizon*, owned by energy company BP, exploded and began leaking oil into the Gulf of Mexico. By the time the underwater oil well was sealed in July 2010, approximately five million barrels of oil had been dumped into the

Sacred Ground

Nanih Waiya is a location in Winston County that the Choctaw tribe considers sacred as the place of origin of their people. The state of Mississippi maintained ownership of the land until 2008, when it was given back to the Choctaw. The tribe holds a yearly celebration of Choctaw culture at Nanih Waiya.

Giving Back

After musician Elvis Presley became famous worldwide, he became known for his charitable acts and made many donations to support his native Mississippi. In 1957, he held a benefit concert to help Tupelo build a new youth center. He also gave a 1975 concert to benefit the victims of a tornado in McComb.

ocean, according to US government estimates. The spill covered vast areas of the Gulf, and it had a long-lasting impact on the water, plants, and animals that live on the Mississippi coast. Oil coated the skin and feathers of birds and sea turtles and caused chemical burns, ulcers and internal bleeding in dolphins, whales, and other mammals. A large number of dolphins and whales died in the year following the spill. The fishing industry is one of the most important aspects of the economy of Gulf Coast states, and it had already faced major challenges after Hurricane Katrina. The oil spill caused further problems for these businesses, as many fish and shellfish were found to be unsafe to eat—and even when the fish were deemed safe, fewer people wanted to buy and eat them after seeing the disaster in the news.

Tourism, another important part of the economy in Mississippi, also took a hit as far fewer people chose to vacation in the area and enjoy the beaches of the Gulf Coast. A chemical used to clean the oil off the surface of the water called Corexit was also found to be toxic. Compounds from this chemical were found in the shells, skin, and flesh of fish, birds, and animals in the region. The oil and chemicals from the spill also affected the health of humans on the Gulf Coast in great numbers. Workers who helped clean up the mess, as well as those who simply lived in the area, faced health problems such as breathing issues, serious headaches, and mental illnesses. Although the oil was cleaned from the water's surface, researchers are continuing to find significant amounts of oil on the Gulf floor. Scientists believe the oil spill will have an impact on the health of the Gulf Coast's ecosystem for years to come.

In Their Own Words

"A house divided against itself cannot stand. I believe this government cannot endure, permanently half slave and half free. I do not expect the Union to be dissolved—I do not expect the house to fall—but I do expect it will cease to be divided."
—President Abraham Lincoln, in a June 16, 1858 speech

★ 10 KEY DATES IN STATE HISTORY ★

1. 1540

Spaniard Hernando de Soto leads the first group of Europeans across what is present-day Mississippi on a search for treasure.

2. May 1, 1699

The French complete the building of Fort Maurepas, the first French settlement in what will become Mississippi, on the northeast shore of Biloxi Bay.

3. April 30, 1803

The Louisiana Purchase opens the Mississippi River to American trade. The United States paid $15 million to France for the territory.

4. March 1, 1817

President James Madison signed legislation enabling residents of the Mississippi Territory to form a state government and be admitted to the Union as the twentieth state.

5. January 9, 1861

The Mississippi secession convention votes to have the state become the second in the South to secede from the Union.

6. August 29, 1939

Oil is discovered near Tinsley, in Yazoo County. It became the first oil field in the state of Mississippi.

7. July 2, 1964

Congress passes the Civil Rights Act, outlawing segregation in public places. Fannie Lou Hamer helps to organize Freedom Summer, an effort to register African-American voters in Mississippi.

8. August 29, 2005

Deadly and destructive Hurricane Katrina makes its first landfall before hitting Mississippi, Louisiana, Alabama, Florida, and parts of Texas.

9. May 10, 2011

Rising waters destroy hundreds of homes in Mississippi as record-breaking flooding along the Mississippi River continues over multiple days.

10. February 7, 2013

Mississippi ratifies the Thirteenth Amendment, abolishing slavery, after it is discovered the state had never filed paperwork with the National Archive to make the amendment official.

The Clarksdale Caravan Blues Festival in 2015 drew talented musicians like fifteen-year-old Christone Kingfish Ingram.

The People

F ive hundred years ago, only Native Americans lived in the region that would later become Mississippi. Even after European explorers reported that the land had the possibility of becoming a bountiful place to live, few white settlers came. When some French settlers arrived in 1699, they settled near present-day Biloxi. The area seemed to offer a natural port for shipping, rich soil for farming, and fresh drinking water in its rivers.

By the early 1700s, Native Americans shared the land with just a few French neighbors. The second French settlement in the area was founded in 1716. Everything changed when the French brought in slaves from Africa. Slaves who could work the land without pay changed the area's fortunes and population. With free labor, the land could be farmed for great profit. This possibility attracted the interest of Great Britain, Spain, and France. Great Britain already had settlers in the Northeast and Spain had settlers in the Southwest. Soon Great Britain and France were fighting over land claims. France finally gave up its land claims to Great Britain after losing the French and Indian War in 1763.

During the short period between that war and the outbreak of the American Revolution, most of the settlers who arrived in the area came from England, Ireland,

A young Choctaw dancer performs at a festival on the reservation near Philadelphia, Mississippi.

Scotland, and Wales. Spain also sent settlers to America. During the Revolution, Spain took the opportunity to seize control of West Florida, which contained part of present-day Mississippi.

After the United States gained its independence from Great Britain in 1783, the population grew quickly. Native Americans, white settlers from Europe, and slaves from Africa made up the population. Newcomers kept arriving in great numbers.

By 1800, about 7,000 Native Americans still lived in what is now Mississippi. In the Natchez area alone, the population numbered between 4,000 and 5,000 whites and blacks, which made it a sizeable city for its time. Approximately 1,200 white settlers and slaves lived along the Tombigbee River.

Increasing numbers of white settlers pushed Native Americans from the territories where they had lived for thousands of years. In 1816, one traveler reported that 4,000 settlers came to the Mississippi River area in just nine days. Between 1810 and 1820, the population soared from approximately 37,000 people to about 75,000 people, including slaves. By 1860, the population had grown to nearly 800,000 people. On the eve of the Civil War, Mississippi's population was about evenly divided between black and white people.

Growth slowed significantly after the end of slavery weakened the economy. New settlers found other parts of the United States more attractive than the southern United States. By 1900, Mississippi had just over 1.5 million people. Between 1910 and 1920, the population actually decreased by several thousand. Mississippi's population went through a series of small increases followed by small decreases over the next few decades. In 2010, over 2.9 million people lived in the state. And while the population is growing, it has remained relatively small compared to other states. For example, the state of Mississippi's population is just slightly higher than that of the city of Chicago.

African Americans made up the majority of Mississippi's population until 1940. Today, however, about 60 percent of Mississippi's population is white. African Americans make up approximately 37 percent of Mississippians. The state has the highest percentage of black people of any state.

In 2010, almost 26,000 Asians and Asian Americans lived in Mississippi. This includes many Filipinos (people from the Philippines) and Vietnamese people who have recently moved to the state. Many came to work in Mississippi's fishing and shrimping industries, while others worked in other Mississippi industries.

The number of Hispanics is increasing rapidly in Mississippi. In 2010 there were more than 81,000 Hispanic residents. Many of them are Mexican Americans or Mexicans who

Hispanic families make up one of the fastest growing ethnic groups in Mississippi.

★ 10 KEY PEOPLE ★ ★ ★

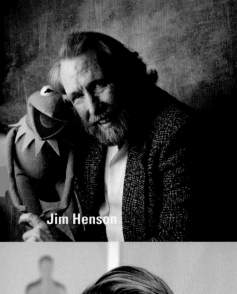

Medgar Evers

Jim Henson

Faith Hill

1. Lacey Chabert

Born in Purvis in 1982, Lacy Chabert began her acting career in community performances in Mississippi. She is known for her roles in *Mean Girls*, *Party of Five*, and as the voice of Eliza Thornberry in *The Wild Thornberrys*.

2. Medgar Evers

Medgar Evers was born in Decatur in 1925. His rejection from the University of Mississippi Law School highlighted the school's segregation policies. Evers, a leader in the civil rights movement, was assassinated by a white supremacist in 1963.

3. William Faulkner

Winner of the 1949 Nobel Prize in Literature, William Faulkner was not only born and raised in Mississippi, he also used the state as the setting in many of his novels. He grew up in Oxford, which he renamed Jefferson in his writing.

4. Jim Henson

Jim Henson was born in 1936 in Greenville and was raised in Leland. He created the *Sesame Street* Muppets. Henson died in 1990. Leland has opened a Jim Henson museum honoring his work.

5. Faith Hill

Born in Jackson in 1967 as Audrey Faith Perry, Faith Hill's career in country music began in the early 1990s. Some of her hit songs include "This Kiss" and "Just to Hear You Say That You Love Me." She is married to singer Tim McGraw.

6. James Earl Jones

James Earl Jones is one of America's most respected film stars. He was born in Arkabutla in 1931. His deep, impressive voice was behind characters such as Mufasa in *The Lion King* and Darth Vader in *Star Wars*.

7. B. B. King

B. B. King, one of the world's great blues musicians, was born in Itta Bena in 1925. He first played the guitar as a child. By the 1950s, he had a long string of hit songs. He died in 2015 at age eighty-nine.

8. Elvis Presley

Elvis Presley, called the King of Rock 'n' Roll, was born in Tupelo in 1935. Elvis had over one hundred songs on the Billboard Hot 100 chart, including "Heartbreak Hotel," "Jailhouse Rock," and "Hound Dog." Elvis died in 1977.

9. James Monroe Trotter

James Trotter was born into slavery in 1842 in Grand Gulf. In 1863 he joined the Fifty-Fifth Massachusetts Regiment and rose to the rank of second lieutenant, one of the first African Americans to achieve that rank.

10. Oprah Winfrey

Oprah Winfrey was born in Kosciusko in 1954 and began working at a radio station while in high school. She hosts a TV show, runs a production company and has written books, published magazines, and donated to many charities.

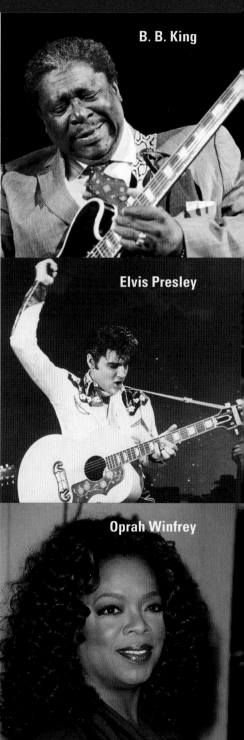

B. B. King

Elvis Presley

Oprah Winfrey

Who Mississippians Are

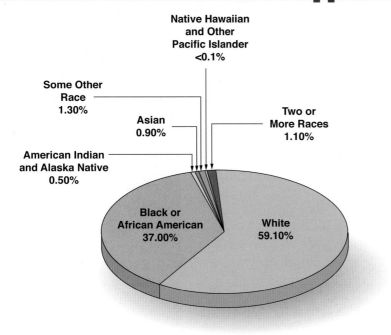

Native Hawaiian and Other Pacific Islander <0.1%

Some Other Race 1.30%

Asian 0.90%

American Indian and Alaska Native 0.50%

Two or More Races 1.10%

Black or African American 37.00%

White 59.10%

**Total Population
2,967,297**

Hispanic or Latino (of any race):
• 81,481 people (2.7 %)

Note: The pie chart shows the racial breakdown of the state's population based on the categories used by the US Bureau of the Census. The Census Bureau reports information for Hispanics or Latinos separately, since they may be of any race. Percentages in the pie chart may not add to 100 because of rounding.

Source: US Bureau of the Census, 2010 Census

have come to the state to work in agriculture. Hispanic populations are growing in Mississippi's cities as well.

In a state with so many agricultural resources, most Mississippians have long chosen to live in rural farming areas. Mississippi's cities have remained small. The largest city, Jackson, has a population of approximately 174,000 people. Biloxi, another major city, is just a quarter of the size of Jackson. Hattiesburg, Meridian, and Gulfport also have populations of slightly more than 40,000. Fewer than 400,000 of the state's residents live in a sizeable city.

Diverse Influences

Today, as in the past, people of diverse origins call Mississippi home. Many of the state's residents have lived in the state all their lives, but Mississippi's population also includes many people who have only recently arrived. Some of these are immigrants, or people who have come from another country to live and to work in the United States. Others have moved to Mississippi from elsewhere in the United States. Some families come because of job opportunities. Many people who move to Mississippi are retirees. They come to spend their later years enjoying the state's restful environment, mild climate, and beautiful scenery.

Cultural influences from a variety of ethnic groups can be seen in the state of Mississippi. Native American culture is still visible. Tourists visit the state to see evidence of the great Mound Builder civilization that developed here a thousand years ago. Although the Mound Builders are long gone, their descendants in other Native American groups remain in Mississippi.

Some descendants of the Chickasaw, the Choctaw, and the Natchez who were living there when the French arrived in the sixteenth century continue to live in Mississippi. The current Natchez Native American population is small and scattered throughout the state, as is the Chickasaw. Nevertheless, museums and cultural centers celebrate their heritage. Mississippi has always had a larger number of Choctaw. Today, thousands live on the Choctaw Reservation, located on Highway 16, in the middle of the state near the town of Philadelphia.

Despite the early Spanish explorations, little of that Spanish influence remains visible today. The French, who followed the Spaniards into the area, left their mark in a few place names, such as Bienville and Bay St. Louis. Louisville was named after France's King Louis XIV. As recently as one hundred years ago, so many people of French descent still lived in the state that French classes were taught in most Mississippi schools. According to one historian, "many people born in the early twentieth century can recall relatives who spoke only or mainly French."

One can also see a few signs of Asian influence in Mississippi. The Chinese, who came to work on cotton plantations in the nineteenth century after the slaves were freed, formed a tightly knit group. One group, from China's Sze Yap district, first lived in Washington County. Later on, another group owned land in Bolivar County. A few Chinese grocery stores can be found around Mississippi. The town of Greenville has a separate Chinese cemetery. Today you can also see store signs written in Vietnamese in Biloxi and other places along the coast where Vietnamese people work as shrimpers. One of the most significant changes in Mississippi's population in recent years has been in the number of Asian Americans living there.

Throughout Mississippi's history, African Americans have had a big influence on life in the state. Many own farms and businesses. Some are active in politics. Particularly in

In Their Own Words

"The beautiful thing about learning is nobody can take it away from you."
—B. B. King

the Delta Region, African-American musicians created a unique kind of music called the blues. Some of this music has a haunting, mournful sound, while some blues songs are lively and fast. Once a branch of folk music, the blues has greatly influenced other types of music, especially rock and roll.

Mississippi for Visitors

Mississippians cherish their heritage. They have preserved many of the state's elegant old homes and neighborhoods. Historical sites also include reminders of difficult times in Mississippi's history, particularly its years of slavery and the Civil War. A historical marker at the site of Natchez's Forks of the Road notes the location of a slave market. Civil War buffs can visit many of Mississippi's battle sites, some of which have been turned into parks or posted with historical markers. Some Civil War groups stage reenactments of famous battles.

Many Mississippians also enjoy sports and the outdoors. Along with out-of-state tourists, they flock to the state's parks, waterways, and other natural areas. Many Mississippians like to hunt, fish, and hike. The state boasts more than fifty state wildlife management areas, fourteen national wildlife refuges, and six national forests. Visitors to the Panther Swamp National Wildlife Refuge, for example, can observe American alligators, otters, swamp rabbits, and minks living in the wild. Visitors to the Gulf Islands National Seashore can sunbathe, swim, or enjoy boating along the white beaches and

Reminders of the Civil War are everywhere in Mississippi.

sparkling ocean. **Coastal marshes** are popular places for hikers. Mississippi's many rivers, lakes, bayous, and oceans are paradises for the state's fishermen and women.

Many residents of Mississippi are avid sports fans. Residents closely follow the teams at the state universities, including the University of Mississippi (or Ole Miss) Rebels and the Mississippi State Bulldogs.

Eating in this top agricultural and fishing state is a delicious experience for Mississippians and tourists alike. The town of Belzoni is often called the farm-raised catfish capital of the world. About 60 percent of the farm-raised catfish in the US are grown near Belzoni. Fried catfish is a favorite dish throughout the state. Mississippi is famous for its dark, rich soil and for its Mississippi mud pies. These thick, gooey chocolate pies resemble the state's thick, dark mud seen in swamps, riverbanks, and bottomlands. Visitors can find sweet potato dishes on restaurant menus throughout the state, which is a major sweet potato grower. Sweet potato pie is a special favorite at Thanksgiving around the country but especially in Mississippi. The town of Vardaman, which calls itself the "Sweet Potato Capital of the World," honors its favorite crop every November. Visitors sample all kinds of sweet potatoes and can purchase a cookbook full of sweet potato recipes. The Mississippi shrimp boils are a delicious feature of many outdoor festivals. Shrimp boils are big pots of shrimp along with meats, vegetables, and spices. A special ceremony in Biloxi every May and June honors fishermen and shrimp harvesters who died at sea. A wreath is dropped into the water at the Biloxi Yacht Club pier. A bishop blesses the boats as they participate in a procession. The Biloxi Seafood Festival in September is another seaside celebration. Events include a schooner boat race and shrimp-eating feasts.

Art and music lovers can find museums, galleries, and concert halls all over the state. The fine art museums include the Ohr-O'Keefe Museum of Art in Biloxi, the Walter Anderson Museum of Art in Ocean Springs, the Lauren Rogers Museum of Art in Laurel, and the Mississippi Museum of Art in Jackson.

Classical music lovers attend concerts in Jackson, which has its own symphony, and at colleges and universities around the state. Mississippians listen to great music, not just in concert halls but also in churches, at county fairs, and at family reunions.

Mississippi's many festivals attract families from all around the region to celebrate the state's rich land, history, great food, wonderful music, and colorful art. The town of Tupelo, for example, throws an Elvis Presley festival once a year. In Greenville, music is in the air every September thanks to its many concerts during the Mississippi Delta Blues and Heritage Festival. Musicians celebrate Mississippi's Delta blues tradition with nonstop music during the festival.

★ 10 ★ KEY EVENTS ★ ★

Carnival on the Coast

Cruisin' the Coast

1. Annual World Catfish Festival

Mississippi's catfish are honored each March in Belzoni. The town hosts a fishing competition, a catfish-eating contest, and even a Miss Catfish pageant! More than ten thousand people attend the festival every year.

2. Canton Flea Market

Held each May, this open-air market is made up of approximately one thousand artists and crafters selling their wares on the lawn of the Madison County Courthouse. The flea market was founded in 1965.

3. Carnival on the Coast

These Mardi Gras celebrations are held on the Gulf Coast and in Natchez every year at the beginning of Lent in late winter. People dress up in outrageous costumes and go to more than twenty parades.

4. Christmas in the Pass

For nearly thirty years, Gulf Coast residents have started the holiday season with this festive event in Pass Christian. Christmas in the Pass recently expanded to two days to add activities such as a lighted boat parade.

5. Cruisin' the Coast

Every October, thousands of car enthusiasts head to Biloxi/Gulfport for what organizers call "America's largest block party." Classic, antique, and hot rod vehicles cruise the 30-mile (48 km) stretch of beachside highway to hear live music and eat local food.

MISSISSIPPI

6. Dixie National Livestock Show and Rodeo

The city of Jackson hosts this celebration every January through early February. The event includes a parade, a rodeo, several livestock shows (including one where kids show off the farm animals they have raised), a dance, and more.

7. Mississippi State Fair

In this rich farming state, the fall harvest is celebrated in Jackson every October. One of the South's largest state fairs gives farmers a chance to show off their finest stock animals and produce. There are also carnival rides and food.

8. Natchez Fall Pilgrimage

Reenactments depict life in Natchez before the Civil War during this three-week festival. Attendees tour nineteen restored, furnished mansions. Tour guides are the descendants of the families that once lived there. A similar event is held in the spring.

9. Rivergate Festival

This family-friendly event is the opportunity to celebrate spring in Tunica with live blues, gospel, and country music. The festival is held over one weekend in April. A barbecue contest draws some of the South's best chefs.

10. Slugburger Festival

The slugburger is a favorite treat of residents of Corinth. This July festival celebrates the slugburger, a patty of beef and soybean grits that is deep fried. Attendees also enjoy live music, rides, and plenty of other delicious foods.

Natchez Fall Pilgrimage

Slugburger Festival

The state capitol building in Jackson was built in 1903. It is the third building to house the legislature in the history of Mississippi.

How the Government Works

Mississippi, like other states, has several tiers of government that serve its people at different levels, including federal, state, county, city, and town. There are 131 towns or villages with fewer than one thousand residents.

On the federal level, citizens of every state, including Mississippi, elect two US senators every six years. The number of representatives a state has in the US House of Representatives varies according to the size of the state's population. Mississippi has four representatives. Both senators and representatives work on behalf of all Americans. They also pay special attention to the needs and concerns of the people of their own state. Mississippians also participate in US presidential elections, which are held every four years.

Political History of Mississippi

Mississippi became a state in 1817. When it formally entered the Union as a state, Mississippi needed a state constitution. Political leaders wrote one immediately. Three other versions followed in 1832, 1869, and 1890.

Marchers, protesting the 1964 murder of three civil rights workers who were registering blacks to vote, take their anger to Philadelphia, Mississippi.

The state constitution spells out how the state's government works. Mississippi's constitution, in its current form, provides for a governor and lieutenant governor to be elected every four years. These officials can serve only two terms in their lifetime. The office of governor is the highest in the state. He or she is responsible for seeing that the laws of the state are upheld. He or she can also convene, or bring together, the state legislature and grant pardons. The constitution also spells out which other officers are to be elected rather than appointed. As in other states, Mississippi also has a two-chamber legislature and a court system.

Like other voters in the United States, many Mississippians belong to one of the two major political parties: the Democrats or the Republicans. As in most of the country, the majority of Mississippi's local, state, and national representatives belong to one of those two political groups.

For most of Mississippi's history, the right to vote was restricted to certain people. Women did not win voting rights until the 1920s. In a new state constitution in 1890, Mississippi curbed African Americans' right to vote, though they had been able to vote during the Reconstruction Era. In protests and marches, African Americans, along with many whites, pressured the federal government to pass the Voting Rights Act of 1965. This law gave African Americans the right to vote again in their states.

Branches of Government

The state government in Mississippi is divided into three branches, as in other states.

Executive

The executive branch is charged with preparing budgets and making sure the laws passed by the legislative branch are carried out. This branch includes the governor, lieutenant governor, and other officials such as the secretary of state, treasurer, auditor, and the attorney general.

Legislative

The legislative branch is made up of the state senate, with 52 members, and the House of Representatives, which has 122 members. Its job is to make and pass state laws.

Judicial

At the top of the judicial branch sits the Mississippi Supreme Court, the court of appeals, and trial courts. Lower courts include circuit courts, chancery courts, county courts, justice courts, and municipal or town courts. All the courts rule on matters of state law.

How a Bill Becomes a State Law

The power to make and pass laws in Mississippi involves the governor as well as state legislators elected to one of two "houses." These houses are the state senate and the house of representatives. A senator or a house representative may introduce a bill (a proposed

Haley Barbour served two terms as governor of Mississippi.

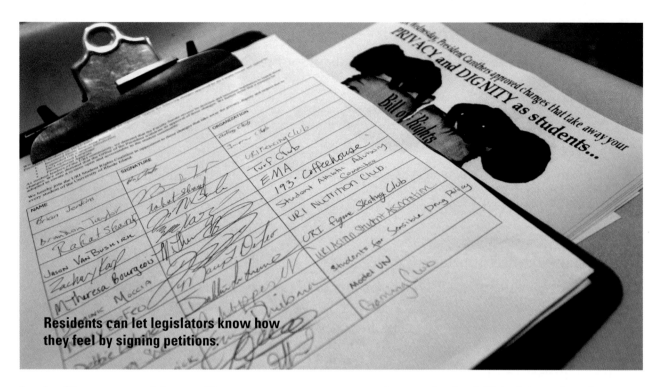

Residents can let legislators know how they feel by signing petitions.

law) of interest to citizens. The senator or representative reads the bill in his or her house. Leaders of that house assign the bill to a committee that specializes in the issue, such as education, transportation, or the environment. The committee studies the bill. When it decides the entire senate or house should hear the bill, the committee schedules a date to do so. After the bill is read, it is put to a vote. If the bill passes in the house where it was read, it is sent to the other house, where the bill goes through the same process.

Bills may be sent back and forth depending on changes that representatives make along the way. Sometimes a bill goes straight to the governor, who signs it into law. However, sometimes the governor vetoes, or refuses to sign, the bill. When that happens, the bill may go back to the senate or the house of representatives for more changes. The governor may then sign it. However, if the governor still vetoes the bill, the legislators can still get it passed. They can override the governor's veto if two-thirds of the members each house vote to pass the bill.

A bill may also go back to the legislature for changes before it ever gets to the governor. At each step, the legislators, including the special committees, must review the changes in the bill before it goes to the governor. The result is called a compromise bill, or one that must satisfy both houses.

The lieutenant governor presides over the state senate and votes if there is a tie. The lieutenant governor can also take over for a governor who is unable to finish his or her term of office.

How Local Government Works

Mississippi is divided into eighty-two counties. Unlike the systems in many other states, an elected five-member board of supervisors runs each county. County boards of supervisors set property taxes. They may decide such matters as which county roads big trucks may travel on, for example. The state also has more than 290 cities and towns with their own local governments. The mayors of most of these cities and towns work with an elected council to make decisions concerning local laws and their enforcement. Mayors and councils pass laws that affect the people who live in their town. They might decide, for instance, where new factories can be built. Such matters are covered by what are called zoning laws.

The Mississippi Band of Choctaw Indians has its own government. Recognized by the US government since 1945, the Choctaw people have their own constitution. It spells out the organization of a Choctaw government council that represents all its members. They also have many government positions similar to those of the US government, including an attorney general, a health department, and fire and law enforcement officials. In 2011, the Mississippi Band of Choctaw Indians elected Phyliss Anderson as its first female tribal chief.

Hot Topics

Just as in other states, political issues come and go in Mississippi. After Hurricane Katrina, residents of the state were concerned about how much help the federal government would be able to provide for rebuilding.

Every day, Mississippians participate in their government and voice their opinions. They write, e-mail, and call their legislators to talk about the issues that concern them. Legislation is often shaped by the voice of the people. By learning about issues, everyone can make a difference.

In 1993, a lawsuit was filed in the Mississippi court system against the governor of the state. The people who filed the lawsuit wanted the state to stop flying the state flag that included part of a Confederate battle flag. A state commission recommended that a new flag be designed and voted on by Mississippians. A majority of the people voted to keep the flag as it was. Many people continue to sign petitions to get the state to change the flag. In June 2015, several prominent lawmakers joined in the call for a redesign.

This kind of public activism keeps Mississippians involved in their government. Mississippians decide their future by their votes and by reminding the people they elect to listen to their voices.

POLITICAL FIGURES
FROM MISSISSIPPI

Jefferson Davis: US Senator, 1847-1851, 1857-1861; President of the Confederate States of America, 1861-1865

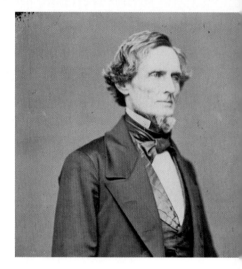

Jefferson Davis argued against secession before the Civil War. When Mississippi left the Union, he resigned his seat in the senate and was elected president of the Confederacy. Davis distinguished himself in the Mexican-American War and served as the US Secretary of War.

Evelyn Gandy: Lieutenant Governor, 1976-1980

Edythe Evelyn Gandy, born in Hattiesburg, was the first woman elected to statewide office in Mississippi when she was picked to be the state's treasurer in 1959. She also served as assistant attorney general and later lieutenant governor under Governor Cliff Finch. She helped pass legislation that created the University of Mississippi Medical Center.

Bennie Thompson: Congressman, 1993-

A native of Bolton, Congressman Thompson has had a long career of supporting civil rights and the advancement of Mississippi's African-American community. As a student at Tougaloo College and Jackson State University, he helped organize voter registration drives for residents of the Mississippi Delta.

MISSISSIPPI
YOU CAN MAKE A DIFFERENCE

Contacting Lawmakers

To contact lawmakers in Mississippi, go to **www.ms.gov** and click on the Government tab. Ask your parents the names of your representatives, then look them up under the Mississippi State Legislature link. To contact US senators and representatives, visit **www.govtrack.us/congress/members/MS** and consult the map to find your district. Then, find the representative from your district listed above the map.

Change of Address

After Hurricane Katrina devastated the Gulf Coast in 2005, many laws and other ways of life in Mississippi changed in order to prevent a similar disaster in the future. The location and height of levees—embankments built to prevent the flooding of a body of water—were changed, and emergency response plans were updated. Thanks to vocal support from the community, lawmakers even passed new legislation that changed a key part of Mississippi's economy—casinos. Before Katrina, laws existed that prevented casinos from being built on land in the state, but it was legal to have them in the water surrounding Mississippi. Casino owners opened floating casinos on barges (large ships) that would dock right off the coast of places like Biloxi and Gulfport. When the hurricane came through, it destroyed almost all of the floating casinos, even washing some of them far onto land. Many people employed by the barge casinos contacted state legislators to say it would be safer and more effective to allow them to exist on land. Casino owners also knew that changing the law would enable them to rebuild as larger, more impressive resorts that could bring new money to the state. Lawmakers acted quickly and in October 2005, a law was passed that made it legal for casinos to be built up to 800 feet (244 m) inland.

Fishing has long been an important
element of the economy of Mississippi.

Making a Living

For hundreds of years, most of Mississippi's wealth came from cotton growing. In fact, cotton made Mississippi one of the richest states in the Union 150 years ago. Today, profits from cotton growing make up a much smaller share of Mississippi's income. In the years between the end of the Civil War and the beginning of World War II, many people in the state struggled to support themselves, as there were few high-paying jobs. Today, however, the situation has changed. The state government and private citizens have made successful efforts to attract new industries to Mississippi.

As in other parts of the United States, most people find employment in the service sector. That means they might work in banks or business offices, for example. Professional service jobs include those held by doctors, nurses, and lawyers. Tens of thousands of other people in the state hold some kind of government job, working for the federal, state, or local government. These people teach, govern, or work in state agencies—some as social workers, administrators, and managers, for example. Tourism is a major industry that creates many other kinds of service jobs in hotels, restaurants, casinos, and major tourists sites. Other workers manufacture goods in Mississippi's factories.

Agriculture

In some periods, such as the time before the Civil War, Mississippi supported vast farmlands that made some people wealthy. Then war, social changes such as the end of slavery, and agricultural competition altered Mississippi's farm economy. Some Mississippians who grew food and cash crops hit difficult times.

In 1929, the Great Depression began. During this period, the national economy collapsed. Mississippi remained a farming state, but a poor one. In 1936, the state government made an effort to change the nature of the state's economy. It created a new program called Balance Agriculture with

Cotton remains a major crop, but its importance to the state has dropped.

Industry. In the years that followed, more and more factories opened across the state. These included furniture and clothing manufacturers that could take advantage of Mississippi's lumber and cotton industries. Today, the people of Mississippi make their living in a variety of ways. Agriculture remains the state's most important economic base. Cotton is still a major industry in Mississippi, with more than 1 million acres (404,686 ha) planted each year. Cotton plants yield cotton bolls, which are picked and then pulled apart to make thread that can then be woven into fabric. Cottonseeds can also be crushed to make oil and shortening used in food processing. Cottonseed feed is used for livestock.

Although cotton remains a major crop, farmers also grow different kinds of crops. Beginning around the 1930s, they began to produce large amounts of soybeans, for example, and crops used for livestock feed. Today, Mississippi has become known for its sweet potatoes, as well as for its pecans, which grow in the state's many orchards. In northern Mississippi, farmers plant about 20,000 acres (8,094 ha) of sweet potatoes each year. Everyone agrees that sweet potatoes grown in the rich soils of northern Mississippi are especially good. Their sales bring close to $82 million into the state economy every year. Soybeans have become one of Mississippi's biggest crops in recent years. About 1.8 million acres (728,434 ha) are planted each year, bringing in around $860 million in production value. Soybeans are major ingredients in livestock feed. They can also be made into products such as tofu, soy milk, and soybean oil.

Other major crops include rice, hay, wheat, and corn. Livestock and livestock products contribute to Mississippi's yearly farm income. Chickens and beef cattle are the state's most valuable livestock. Mississippi usually ranks among the top five states in producing chickens, called broilers. Farmers also sell large numbers of hogs and chicken eggs as well as substantial amounts of dairy products. In the 1940s, Mississippi farmers started to raise chickens on a large scale. Today, the state has about two thousand poultry farms producing 757 million broilers each year. Mississippi is also home to the largest egg processing company in the world.

Fishing

Taking advantage of their state's abundant inland waters, many Mississippians make their money from catfish farms. Mississippi leads all states in the production of freshwater catfish on farms. Beginning in the 1960s, many farmers whose land had been overused for cotton growing decided to try something new. They began to dig ponds for raising catfish. Today, the state exports millions of pounds of the fish every year.

Mississippians also fish the state's rivers and lakes and harvest shrimp and oysters off the state's southern coast. Pascagoula-Moss Point is one of the nation's leading fishing ports. Biloxi is the state's chief shrimp port.

Natural disasters have made fishing for a living much harder in Mississippi.

★ 10 KEY★INDUSTRIES

Catfish

Cotton

1. Agriculture

Mississippi's warm and moist climate makes it ideal for growing many crops and raising farm animals. Silt from the Mississippi River makes the soil rich with nutrients. The state has more than 11 million acres (4,451,542 ha) of farmland.

2. Casinos

Casinos, where people can gamble, were legalized in Mississippi in 1990. Since then, they have grown to become a major part of the state's economy. Some residents believe casinos encourage gambling addiction and illegal activity.

3. Catfish

Mississippi began commercially raising catfish in 1965 and since then has grown to become the country's largest producer of this fish. Catfish are a hearty fish that thrive in a farmed environment.

4. Cotton

Cotton has played a key role in Mississippi's economy since the state's earliest days. Advances in agriculture have improved cotton farming. Scientists breed cotton plants that are hardier and easier to grow.

5. Fishing

Thanks to its location on the Gulf of Mexico, Mississippi's fishing industry has a large impact on the state's economy. Catfish, oysters, blue crabs, and shrimp are major products from the Gulf and Mississippi Delta.

MISSISSIPPI ★ ★ ★

6. Manufacturing

Many products are made or assembled by Mississippi manufacturers, including navy ships, cars and tires, furniture, and medical devices. In addition to traditional factories, there are many advanced manufacturing companies located in Mississippi.

7. Oil and Gas

In 2011, the US Department of Energy reported that more than 24 million barrels (3,815,695,200 L) of crude oil were produced in Mississippi, making it fourteenth in the nation for oil production.

8. Soybeans

Soybeans are a top crop in Mississippi. The soybean is easy to grow, has protein and vitamins, and can be used to make other products like feed for farm animals. Using crop engineering, Mississippi farmers are growing more soybeans than ever.

9. Sweet Potatoes

Sweet potatoes have been growing in America's southeastern region since 1648. In 2012, 104 commercial sweet potato growers planted 22,400 acres (9,065 ha) in Mississippi.

10. Rice

This staple food is grown in large amounts in Mississippi. Most rice farms are located in the northeastern part of the state. Most Mississippi rice farmers grow long-grain rice. About 200,000 acres (80,937 ha) of rice are planted here each year.

Oil and Gas

Sweet Potatoes

Recipe for Cheesy Sweet Potatoes

Sweet potatoes are a favorite food of Mississippi natives. They are rich in flavor when roasted or baked and full of vitamins and fiber. Work with an adult to follow this recipe for a delicious side dish.

What You Need

4 small sweet potatoes; cut in half lengthwise

2 tablespoons (30 mL) olive oil

1 cup (237 mL) shredded cheese
(parmesan and mozzarella work well;
mix two or more kinds for extra flavor)

Salt and pepper

Watercress for garnish (optional)

What To Do

- Preheat the oven to 425°F (218°C). Ask an adult for help with the oven.
- Rub the olive oil on the potatoes.
- Sprinkle the potatoes with salt and pepper.
- Place the potatoes cut-side down on a baking sheet and bake for eighteen to twenty-two minutes. They should be golden brown and tender when you poke them with a fork.
- Ask an adult to turn the oven to broil.
- Combine the cheese (if using more than one kind) in a bowl.
- Turn the potatoes over and sprinkle with cheese.
- Broil until the cheese melts and is slightly brown (about three minutes.)
- Let cool and enjoy!

Lumbering

Thanks to its extensive forests, Mississippi typically ranks among the ten leading states that produce forestry products. Mississippi farmers grow some of the nation's Christmas trees. Forest products also include pine and hardwood lumber as well as pulpwood, which is used to make paper. The state's superior lumber has led to the development of factories that make furniture and other wood products. Over two hundred furniture companies in the northeastern corner of Mississippi produce furniture from local lumber cut in the state's sawmills. Since the early 1990s, many new jobs in the state were in the furniture and wood products industry.

Manufacturing

Mississippi not only grows cotton, but its textile mills and clothing manufacturers turn that cotton into fabric and clothing right in the state. Other Mississippi factories produce packaged foods, paint, transportation equipment, and electronic equipment. More than six thousand people work in Mississippi's chemical industry. Some of the chemicals are made from the state's oil and mineral resources.

The forests of Mississippi provide wood for carvers and furniture makers.

Workers in some of Mississippi's factories produce aerospace equipment and motor vehicle parts. Factories in Tupelo, Columbus, Jackson, and Natchez produce wood products. Corinth and Jackson are the chief centers for producing electronic equipment. Meatpacking, poultry processing, the manufacturing of cheese, and the canning and freezing of fish are important food industries. Other items manufactured in Mississippi include industrial machinery, chemicals, fabricated metal products, and refined petroleum. Today, the state is a leader in the telecommunications industry, with more than 300,000 miles (482,803 km) of fiber optic cables placed in the ground.

Oil and Gas

A long time ago, seas covered all of Mississippi. When the water receded, rich deposits of petroleum and minerals were left behind. In 1939, the news broke that an oil well in Yazoo County had begun to produce. By 1970, the state's wells numbered in the thousands, which together yielded more than 65 million barrels (over 10 billion liters) of oil every year. Another of the state's natural resources is natural gas, which can be used to generate electricity. Mississippi has hundreds of oil and gas fields and is one of the top fifteen oil-producing states. Today, there are several thousand wells that produce millions of barrels of oil each year.

Other materials mined in Mississippi include sand, gravel, crushed stone, and limestone, as well as clay, marl, cement rock, sandstone, bentonite, and fuller's earth, a kind of clay used in processing certain oils.

New Horizons

For a long time, Mississippi's economy was slow to grow. Over the last several decades, though, the state's leaders have worked hard to change that. One way they have done so is to attract tourists and retired people to their state. Each year, several million travelers come to Mississippi to enjoy its natural beauty and warm weather. While visiting, they spend money by staying in hotels and motels, buying gas for their cars, and eating out at restaurants. The annual economic benefit of tourism to the state is nearly $6 billion.

Natural Destruction

The Great Mississippi Flood of 1927 was the most destructive river flood in the history of the United States. The flood covered more than 23,000 square miles (59,570 sq km) over ten states and led to the construction of the world's longest system of levees and floodways.

Shipyards in Pascagoula perform repairs for the navy and for commercial ships.

Many visitors travel along the Natchez Trace Parkway, which follows the route of the Natchez Trace, an important road in the history of Mississippi and the South that connects Natchez and Nashville, Tennessee. Other National Park Service areas in the state are Brices Cross Roads National Battlefield Site near Tupelo, Gulf Islands National Seashore, Tupelo National Battlefield, and Vicksburg National Military Park.

Looking to the Future

Almost every Mississippi industry was affected in some way by Hurricane Katrina in 2005, and it has taken several years for the state to fully recover. Mississippi received another blow in 2010 when the *Deepwater Horizon* oil rig exploded in the Gulf of Mexico. For nearly three months, oil gushed into the Gulf and made its way to the state's beaches. Marine life in the Gulf was damaged and the state's tourism industry suffered. However, the people of Mississippi came together to do all they could to protect their state. Today, tourists and Mississippians alike can once again enjoy the state's beautiful beaches and wildlife.

Mississippians have endured many hard times. However, they continue to rebuild their state with determination and strength. They are committed to making their state better than ever!

MISSISSIPPI
STATE MAP

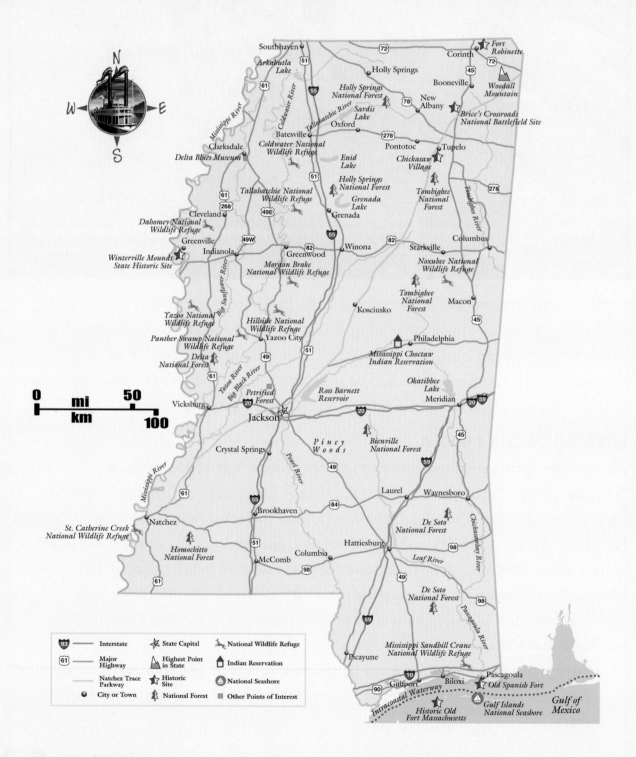

Southhaven

Arkabutla Lake

Holly Springs

Corinth

Fort Robinette

72

51

61

Coldwater River

55

Holly Springs National Forest

Tallahatchie River

Booneville

45

New Albany

78

Woodall Mountain

Batesville

Oxford

Sardis Lake

278

Pontotoc

Tupelo

Brice's Crossroads National Battlefield Site

Clarksdale

Delta Blues Museum

Coldwater National Wildlife Refuge

Enid Lake

Chickasaw Village

Mississippi River

51

Holly Springs National Forest

Tombigbee National Forest

278

61

268

Tallahatchie National Wildlife Refuge

Grenada Lake

Grenada

Tombigbee River

Cleveland

49E

Dahomey National Wildlife Refuge

Greenville

49W

Indianola

55

Winona

82

Starkville

Columbus

Winterville Mounds State Historic Site

Big Sunflower River

Greenwood

82

Noxubee National Wildlife Refuge

Morgan Brake National Wildlife Refuge

45

Yazoo National Wildlife Refuge

Hillside National Wildlife Refuge

Kosciusko

Tombigbee National Forest

Macon

Panther Swamp National Wildlife Refuge

Yazoo City

51

Philadelphia

Delta National Forest

49

Yazoo River

Big Black River

61

Mississippi Choctaw Indian Reservation

Okatibbee Lake

Petrified Forest

Ross Barnett Reservoir

Meridian

20

59

Vicksburg

20

Jackson

20

45

Crystal Springs

Piney Woods

Bienville National Forest

59

Pearl River

49

Laurel

Waynesboro

Mississippi River

61

55

84

Brookhaven

Chickasawhay River

Natchez

De Soto National Forest

St. Catherine Creek National Wildlife Refuge

Homochitto National Forest

51

Columbia

Hattiesburg

98

Leaf River

McComb

98

De Soto National Forest

49

98

61

Pascagoula River

59

Mississippi Sandhill Crane National Wildlife Refuge

Picayune

Pascagoula

Old Spanish Fort

10

Gulfport

Biloxi

90

Intracoastal Waterway

Historic Old Fort Massachusetts

Gulf Islands National Seashore

Gulf of Mexico

Legend

93	Interstate	★ State Capital	⧨ National Wildlife Refuge	
61	Major Highway	▲ Highest Point in State	⌂ Indian Reservation	
	Natchez Trace Parkway	★ Historic Site	⛺ National Seashore	
●	City or Town	♠ National Forest	■ Other Points of Interest	

Scale

0 — mi — 50
km
100

MISSISSIPPI
MAP SKILLS

1. Which city shown on the map is located closest to Hillside National Wildlife Refuge?

2. If you traveled west on Highway 20 from Jackson, which city would you reach?

3. The highest point of the state is located on which mountain?

4. If you were in Southaven and traveled south, which body of water would you reach first?

5. Which national forest can be found southeast of Hattiesburg?

6. According to the map, which three cities can be found on the Gulf of Mexico?

7. Using the map scale, measure approximately how many miles separate Winona from Starkville.

8. Which river runs through Batesville?

9. The Petrified Forest is located northwest of which major city?

10. What is the name of the fort located closest to the northeast corner of the state?

Arkabutla Lake

De Soto National Forest

1. Yazoo City
2. Vicksburg
3. Woodall Mountain
4. Arkabutla Lake
5. De Soto National Forest
6. Biloxi, Gulfport, and Pascagoula
7. 50 miles
8. Tallahatchie River
9. Jackson
10. Fort Robinette

State Flag, Seal, and Song

The Mississippi flag, adopted in 1894, has a square in the corner with thirteen stars in a blue ×. These are said to represent the thirteen original colonies of the United States. During the period when the South formed the Confederate States of America, the stars represented the eleven Southern states in the Confederacy plus Kentucky and Missouri. The three bars on the rest of the flag are blue, white, and red.

In the center of Mississippi's state seal is an eagle. Across its chest lies a shield, with stars at the top and stripes down below. The eagle, with widespread wings, clasps both an olive branch and arrows in its talons. This symbolizes that the state desires peace but is prepared to fight.

The state song is "Go, Mississippi!" with words and music by Houston Davis. It was adopted in 1962. There was no official state song before then. See the lyrics at **www.50states.com/songs/miss.htm**.

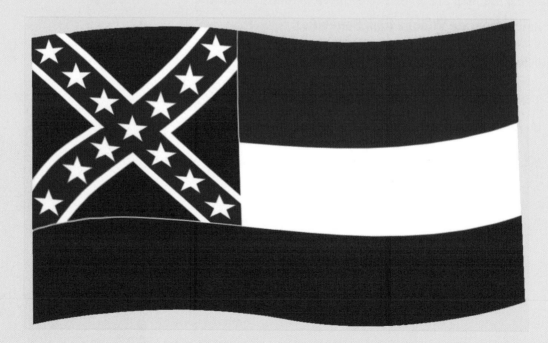

Glossary

archaeologist   A scientist who studies human history by digging up artifacts and other ancient objects.

barge   A flat-bottom boat that carries large amounts of goods, usually on canals and rivers.

coastal marsh   A low-lying area on the edge of land, usually covered with water and full of reeds and tall grasses.

debate   A formal discussion in a meeting or a legislative body in which opposing arguments are expressed.

delta   An area, usually triangular, where a major river divides into smaller rivers before flowing into an ocean. The soil in these areas is usually rich in nutrients.

ethnologist   A scientist who studies human beings, including our history and the way we live our lives now.

levees   An embankment, similar to a dam, that is constructed next to a body of water to prevent flooding.

Louisiana Purchase   The name of the 1803 agreement in which the United States purchased a large section of land from France for $15 million.

minko   A word in the Choctaw language used to refer to a chief or leader of the tribe.

secede   To withdraw formally from a federal union, country, or alliance.

segregation   The forced separation of different racial groups in a community.

sharecroppers   Farmers who rented land to raise crops and received a portion of what was raised, while the remaining crops were owned by the landowner.

Tories   Residents of the colonies who supported the British during the American Revolution.

venomous   Describing insects or animals, usually snakes, that can inject a toxic substance, known as venom, with a bite or a sting.

More About Mississippi

BOOKS

Holling, Holling Clancy. *Minn of the Mississippi*. Boston: Houghton Mifflin, 1978.

Marsico, Katie. *The Mississippi River*. Social Studies Explorers: It's Cool to Learn About America's Waterways. Ann Arbor, MI: Cherry Lake Publishing, 2013.

Rubin, Susan Goldman. *Freedom Summer: The 1964 Struggle for Civil Rights in Mississippi*. New York, NY: Holiday House, 2014.

Yasuda, Anita. *What's Great About Mississippi?* Our Great States. Minneapolis, MN: Lerner Publishing Group, 2015.

WEBSITES

Fun Things to Do in Mississippi

visitthedelta.com/attractions/family_fun.aspx

Mississippi Museum of Natural Science

mdwfp.com/museum.aspx

Official State Website of Mississippi

www.ms.gov

Visit Mississippi

visitmississippi.org

ABOUT THE AUTHORS

Ann Graham Gaines is a freelance writer who lives with her children in a cabin in the woods near Gonzales, Texas.

Kerry Jones Waring is a writer and communications professional. She lives in Buffalo, New York, with her husband and son.

Index

Page numbers in **boldface** are illustrations. Entries in **boldface** are glossary terms.

Index